MY LIFE AND TIMES

A Memoir

By

Maribel Savage Edwards

My Life and Times

My name is Maribel Savage. I was born in Sherman, Texas on June 22, 1926. My parents were Maribel Badgett and William Payne Savage.

I was my parent's first child. I was also the first Grandchild and the first Great Grandchild. My Brother, Claude Ray Savage, was born seven years later on July 2, 1933.

When I was born my parents were living on Montgomery St in Sherman, TX. My Father's mother lived next door. In fact, my father's sisters had given him the lot so he would live next door to his mother. That didn't work out too well. The Depression hit and my father changed jobs and moved to Amarillo. He was one of the lucky ones, he had a job.

I remember my Grandmothers house, however, that may be from later visits when I was older. I was three when we moved to Amarillo. I have a vague memory of a Bridge party my mother had. She had put some stuffed prunes on the tables for a snack. A little boy and I ate the stuffing out of all of them.

I remember the first house we moved to in Amarillo. Our car was a green 1929 Chevy. My Mothers Parents had moved to Quitaque about the same time and they had a car just like it.

My Mother's parents had lived in Bells, TX. My Grandfather owned a Drugstore there. The Depression relocated a lot of people. My Grandfather went into partnership with Mr. Gardner and Mr. Russell. Mr. Gardner was another Pharmacist and Mr. Russell was a Ranch owner.

I don't remember special pets from my very early years. There must have been a number of them though. One of the stories I heard most often was how I brought a stray cat home, got ringworm from it, and all my hair came out. I had the reputation of bringing home any cat that crossed my path. I remember having orange Persian cats but there were a number of them over a period of years.

My Mother was a housewife and my Father worked for Morrow-Thomas Hardware in Amarillo. He had worked at Hardwick-Etter Hardware in Sherman. He worked as bookkeeper when we first went to Amarillo. When I was 10 he was given a salesman job and a route over the Panhandle. We moved to Lubbock because that was the center of his territory and he could be gone only one or two nights a week and drive home the other days.

I don't remember my parents having many special friends. They both drank a great deal. This was during Prohibition! I think the drinking played a great part in the breakup of my parents' marriage when I was 13.

When I was 13 and Ray was 5 we were sent to Quitaque to stay with my Grandparents. This was not a strange place because we visited there frequently and spent the summer with them. It would have been easier on me if I had been told this was to be a permanent arrangement. I felt abandoned and I will forever be grateful to my Grandparents. I didn't think they should have to take on the rearing of two children. They had raised their three daughters and the youngest daughter had married just three years before they took us.

My Grandparent's care probably made the difference in my life. They were always patient and caring with us. I was not an easy child to raise, I am sure. I had been told, finally, that we would live with my Grandparents and my Parents would support us. To my knowledge, my father sent two checks, both of which bounced. My Mother went to Business school and then to Washington, DC to work. I don't remember her sending money, not even a Birthday Card. She always said it must have gotten lost in the mail. My Grandfather said the Lost Mail Dept must be full of her letters.

My Grandparents deserve credit for teaching me Morals, Ethics, Compassion and to be the best that I could. I can still hear my Grandfather's voice when I had strayed from the path I should have taken. He never told me to do or not to do anything. He would point out the possible outcome if I continued to do what I was doing. Then he would tell me the possible results if I did something else. He never told me what to do, just to make up my mind what I wanted as an end result. I still repeat those words to myself when I have a problem.

If I add the places I lived as a child and the places I lived after I married, we will both be surprised.

Montgomery St, Sherman, TX
15th St, Amarillo, TX
12th St, Amarillo
11th St, Amarillo downtown
Harrison St, Amarillo,

Bellevue, Amarillo
Hillcrest, Amarillo
16th St., Amarillo
15th St, Lubbock
16th St, Lubbock
26th St, Lubbock   second house my parents built.
Quitaque.
19th St Lubbock- business college
16th Ave Lubbock when I married.
12th St Room Lubbock until RG went to Yale
16th Ave Lubbock until I went to Washington, DC
Washington, DC and stayed with mother until joined RG in New Haven'
Apt in New Haven until transferred to Denver
Pearl St, Denver
Ft Sumner, NM
Riverside, Calif. RG got out of Service at end of WW2
10th St Lubbock
Lubbock AFB Barracks
Room in San Antonio
Garage Apt in San Antonio RG recalled to AF
Trinidad, BWI
Mount Holly, NJ
Vincentown, NJ
Fullilove St, Bossier City, LA
4423 Bay Villa, Tampa, Fl
England, three houses
Springfield, Mass
Fussa Japan 2 houses
Washington, DC
Big Spring, TX
Tampa Bay Villa, retirement.

This is about 40 moves, bet there are more!

Since there was a seven year gap in Ray and my ages, we didn't have much in common. I started High school when he started first grade. He was 10 when I married.

My health was good in my early childhood. I had the usual childhood diseases. Or what used to be the childhood diseases. They seem to have vaccine for most of them now. I had chicken pox about six. I had measles when I was about 7 ½. My Doctor was before his time. When I was convalescing he gave my brother about 30 c.c.s of my blood. Ray had about 10 spots and no other symptom. He was then immune to measles. That was forty years before there was a vaccine.

I had mumps at 10. We moved to Lubbock just as I came down with them.

At 73 I still have my tonsils, adenoids, appendix and everything else that came as original equipment. I have been a hospital patient three times in my life. That was when my two children were born and when I came back from Trinidad. The whole family was hospitalized at Ft Hamilton, NY that time. The ship we were sent back on in 1949 had been moving displaced persons from Europe to Peru. They re routed the ship to pick up our Squadron and families. The ship had not been cleaned and a number of people were ill. We were in the hospital for 10 days. RG, David and I were ill. Robert was put in as a boarder since there was no one to care for him.

I see little similarity in the training of children now and in my childhood. My peers were spanked when they needed it. Now you can go to jail for spanking a child. I wouldn't have dared talk back to my parents, much less be rude to any adult. Now the child is expressing himself.

My generation was expected to take responsibility for mistakes and to make amends. Now it is deny, deny, deny. The child of the 2000s is to blame for nothing. He had a bad childhood or didn't get all the worldly goods due him. My generation had the Depression and then World War Two. In the Depression we had nothing because most people didn't have jobs. In World War Two the money was there but there was nothing to buy. Everything was rationed or non-existent.

I don't remember doing without in the depression. That was probably because my Father always had a job. He was one of few. We made do with leftovers. Clothes were remade and cut down. We learned to feed a family on very little and maintain good health. The fact that we couldn't have every whim satisfied made us appreciate what we did have. We amused ourselves with our imagination, not something expensive from the store.

I started school at age six in Amarillo. Amarillo High School and the Grade school were in the same block. They were a block from my house. My first grade teacher was Miss Jenkins and my second grade teacher was Mrs. Miller. We had moved when I was ready for third grade and I went to Margaret-Wills. I moved several times in that year but was always close enough to go to the same school.

In the middle of the third grade we moved to Lubbock and I went to Central Ward on Ave Q and 13th. It was a very old school. It was the first school in Lubbock. It was two stories and a full basement. There were four rooms on each floor and the restrooms were in the basement with the heating plant and two classrooms. I was intrigued by the fire escapes from the second floor. This was in the days when students went barefoot in the summer months. This was discouraged at Central Ward. The floors were wide wooden boards that had been oiled for generations. They had splinters and must have been a fire hazard. Central Ward was torn down and a Sears Store built on the site in the 50s.

I went to Central Ward the last half of the third grade and the fourth grade. The fifth, sixth and seventh were in Lubbock Junior High on 16th street.

I moved to Quitaque and went to high School there. In that day there were 11 grades and High School was the eighth, ninth, tenth and eleventh. I graduated from Quitaque High in 1943. I was in a class of 19.

I graduated from High School in May and left for Lubbock to go to Draughon's Business College in June.

Mary Joyce Bailey was my roommate and we lived on 19th in Lubbock. Joyce was a year older than I was but had gone to the same High School. We roomed in a home on 19th and ate at a home in the next block. We both started Draughon's School. I finished in a few months and went to work with Aetna Life Insurance Company

Joyce had gone to Texas Tech for a year and knew R. G. there. We were at Wiley's drug store one evening and R. G. came in with some of his friends. By this time he was in the Army Air Force and Stationed at South Plains Army AirField just north of Lubbock.

We dated several months and decided to get married. Since I was 17 and R. G. was 21, World War 2 was at its worst, and no one knew what the future would be I can see why my Grandparents were not too sure we knew what we were doing.

I lived with my Grandparents but my Mother was still my legal Guardian. She called me from Washington and told me I should think it over but that she would not stand in the way if that was what we wanted. No doubt my Grandmother had given her all the details.

We made our Wedding plans and we paid for our Wedding. We had no time for a Honeymoon but spent the next 20 years traveling all over the world.

The War had started in 1941 and some of the boys didn't wait to graduate. Those that did graduate went into the service soon. There were only 11 years in Public School at that time so we were only 16 or 17 when we left school. I was 16 when I graduated and 17 the next month.

Two of my classmates from these years are still in touch. I met Marilyn Wheeler in Central Ward and was in school with her until I left Lubbock. After my parents built the house on 26th we lived two blocks apart. Most of the time we walked to school. This was over a mile but everyone walked. On cold or bad days someone's parent would usually take us to school. There were no school buses unless you lived out in the country. The city bus was available and was used in an emergency.

Lubbock was originally laid out with every 8th block set aside for a city park. That meant a park within walking distance of every child. We were free to go to the park and spend the day in the summer. Some times there was a supervisor but that was to take care of the sports equipment. We were warned about speaking to strangers but it wasn't a serious problem. We were free to walk to movies and spend the afternoon. Sometimes we walked home; sometimes we called a parent to come get us. No one would dare let a child go to a movie alone in this day and time.

I remember going to the High School on 19th street to skate. No child would have damaged anything on the school ground. Vandalism was not a problem.

In Quitaque I remember several classmates. I am still in touch with Bettye Love. She married in our Junior year. I don't know whether she graduated or not. She married a boy from the area. I lost touch with her for several years because she moved to Albuquerque the same time I moved to England and we lost addresses. By this time I didn't have family living in Quitaque.

When I moved to Tampa for the second time Bettye's daughter was in the area and got my address for her mother. We have corresponded regularly ever since.

My best friend in High School was Betty Owens. She was the middle in age of three sisters. She had Polio as a baby and was in the Shriners hospital for surgery nearly every summer. Her health was never good; she lost her hearing about age 20. She died at age 40.

Beth Starkey was a class mate. She was also my roommate when we went to Business School in Lubbock after we graduated from High School. She was my Maid of Honor when I married. She had diabetes from the time she was about thirteen. She died when she was twenty-six. Diabetes was harder to control at that time. She had lost her sight and was an invalid her last two years.

My grades in school were about average. I am afraid I didn't work very had at being a good student. I don't remember having a hard time with any subject, some of them I liked better than others. I took all the math courses in High School because I had an easier time with them.

Being a High School student in World War Two made you a little more serious than you might have been. Grand Dad had never allowed girls to work at the Drug Store because he said the work was too hard for them physically. Since most of the boys had left for service or were needed on their family farms, he finally let girls work there. Mildred Coker started working there the year before I did.

I will never forget the day of my 16th birthday. Grand Dad called the house and told my Grandmother to send me down. He had me fill out the application for Social Security cards and I started working that day. I worked about an hour in the morning, went to school and was allowed to leave about 15 minutes early at noon. That got me to the Drug Store in time for the noon rush. Back to school and when school was out in the afternoon, back to the Drug Store until about 10 PM. I had every third Sunday and Wednesday evening after 6 PM off. That doesn't give you much time to get in trouble. I learned a lot at the Drug Store, about people, business and responsibility. It was hard work but I am grateful for the time I worked there.

I remember my first year of school but I don't remember the first day. My brother, Ray was born in July before I started Second grade in September.

I don't remember the Principal but I remember my first grade teacher, Miss Jenkins. She was small and slender and very soft-spoken. Mrs. Miller, my second grade teacher was a large woman with dark hair. I was very fond of both of them.

I don't remember many of my friends from those years. There was a girl named Amelia that lived in the apartment house in the next block. I used to play with her a lot and was fascinated with the elevator and the underground garage.

My next door neighbor was named Lillian Roach. She was a couple of years older than I was but we played together a lot. Nancy Brent lived across the street. She was a year younger but I spent a lot of time with her. Her mother taught in the High School next door to our grade school. Her father had died of Polio a few years before. Her two maiden aunts lived with her and her mother. I remember the Ford Electric Car they had. I can't see why it is so hard to get an electric car in 2000 when in 1930 they were very popular.

I moved to Lubbock at mid-term in the third grade. I met Marilyn Wheeler in Central Ward and we have remained friends all these years.

In Eighth grade I moved to Quitaque and Sissy (Betty) Owens became my constant companion. I was always a little jealous. She ate everything she wanted and never gained an ounce. Her whole family was tall and slender. I watched what I ate and gained steadily.

I have often wondered how life would have been different if the Second World War had not started for the USA in 1941. Most of the boys in town went into the service as soon as they were out or school or old enough. The girls left for school or jobs to help with the war. Most of them never came back to their hometowns. The boys married and settled where their wives families lived or in an area they had been stationed in the Military. The girls stayed in towns they had worked in or married in.

I finished High School in May of 1943. I went to Lubbock to Draughon's Business School. Strangely enough, my mother had gone there after she was divorced and before she moved to Washington, D. C.

I married in the summer of 1944. RG had been in the service for about two years. He had applied for Cadet training and had waited 19 months for the assignment to come through. We married Saturday night and his orders were on the Major's desk Monday morning.

Wedding

Joyce knew R. G. in Tech and introduced him to me. We were at Wiley's drug store one evening and R. G. came in with some of his friends. By this time he was in the Army Air Force and Stationed at South Plains Army Air Field just north of Lubbock.
Joyce knew R. G. in Tech and introduced him to me. We were at Wiley's drug store one evening and R. G. came in with some of his friends. By this time he was in the Army Air Force and Stationed at South Plains Army airfield just north of Lubbock.

We were married in the home of the Assistant Pastor of the First Methodist Church in Lubbock. The Pastor was a childhood friend of R G's. Since we had the choice of inviting the entire Squadron RG was assigned to or having a small family wedding, we chose a small home wedding. It was also Easter Weekend and the church didn't have a lot of free time. My Grandparents and brother Ray came for the wedding. R. G.'s parents came to visit the next day and we had lunch with them.

Beth Starkey was my Maid of Honor and Dave Kolick was RG's Best Man. After the ceremony we went to our favorite Mexican Food Restaurant for dinner.

R. G. always said we didn't have a honeymoon since it was wartime and he was leaving for Yale. I don't agree with that. The next 30 years were a honeymoon. How many people do you know that spent 20 years touring 3 continents? We stayed long enough in each place to be a resident instead of a visitor. It is amazing how much you learn about people when they know you long enough to consider you a neighbor.

Washington, D. C.

R. G. left for Yale and I left for Washington, D. C. to work for the Corp of Engineers. I had finished Draughon's and was working in Lubbock for Aetna Life Insurance Company when we married.

During the War the Government sent recruiters all over the country trying to get people to come to Washington, D. C. to take jobs. Since my Mother was already there working for the State Department it seemed like a good thing to do.

I left in May for Washington. I took the train from Lubbock to Washington. At my Grandparents urging I stayed with my Mother. She lived in an apartment on Rhode Island Ave, sharing the apartment with a widow. It was crowded so my mother and I moved to a furnished room.

I went to work at the Pentagon for training and was assigned to the Corp of Engineers. The Engineers had a new building and it is now the State Department.
My Mother worked at the old State Department next door to the Whitehouse and that is now the Offices of the President.

My Mother worked in the Far East Division of State. Her boss was assigned to China. He promised her that he would transfer her to China. She always had a great desire to see the Orient. China fell to the Japanese about the time her boss, George Atcheson, was killed in a plane crash on the way back from China. It seems strange that she always wanted to see the Orient and I spent three years in Japan. She would have enjoyed it.

After my Mother and I moved to the room we were close enough to walk to work if the weather was nice. I remember one morning on the way to work, as I crossed Pennsylvania Ave, I saw a man standing on the steps of Blair House waving to the people passing by. It took me a few minutes to realize that it was Winston Churchill. The news never mentioned any facts that might help the enemy. The location of Churchill could have been important.

A few weeks later I was told to go to the pass section a few blocks away. My pass needed updating. As I got to Constitution Ave. A car was pulling out with a very tall, thin man in it. He had the French military hat on. That was my one glimpse of DeGaul.

I was not in Washington long enough to do much sight seeing. It was not a place to sight see in Wartime.

R. G. finally found a two-room apartment in New Haven. I quit my job and joined him.

He was stationed in Sterling Hall at Yale. It is just across the street from a very old cemetery. A lot of the graves were from the 1600s.

The Green in New Haven has three churches on it. I was impressed with the fact that they paved the paths people made cutting across lawn instead of making sidewalks and expecting people to stay on them. Center Church had a Cemetery below it. I think the cemetery was there first and the Church built over it.

The Cadet program was hard on students. They were pushed as hard as possible to learn their subject in as short a time as possible. RG looked like a skeleton, he never could eat in a hurry and they had 15 minutes for each meal.

He passed out at parade one morning and was sent to the East Haven Hospital. Most of his treatment was feeding him and making up the weight he had lost. Since he had not failed academically the Government had to let him finish his course. He and six other cadets were transferred to Lowry Field in Denver, Colo when the Cadet program was closed at Yale.

Denver

R. G. was studying Aerial Photography. When he got to Lowry they got to the flying training. They literally hung out of the open bomb bays with Speed Graphic Cameras and took their pictures. Denver being cold, plus the altitude and open Bomb Bays in the middle of winter was not the most comfortable place to be. I still have some of the Yale and Denver pictures.

We had a furnished room on the third floor of a house in Denver. I spent a lot of time walking nine blocks to the main road and taking a bus to Lowry and seeing a movie or having dinner with RG.

I remember the beautiful Library in Denver and the Rocky Mountains that you could always see in the distance.

Graduation day finally arrived in February of 1945. The seven remaining Cadets and their families, if they had family there, met in the Commanders office. They had their first gold bars pinned on.

Tradition says that you give the first person that salutes you a dollar bill. I remember as we left the building a young GI passed and saluted. When RG called him back I felt sorry for him. He was sure he had done something wrong. They were not used to having new officers there so he was surprised.

Ft. Sumner, N M

I was pregnant with David. He was due in May. We left by train and went to Ft Sumner, N M. The new Lt. were given a list of the available assignments and decided among themselves where they would go. Ft Sumner was about 200 miles from Olton, TX where RG's parents lived.

We had a three-room apartment on the hill between Ft Sumner and the Air Force Base. It was part of a building that had three apartments. We used to go for long walks or go to the base movie. That was about the size of it. The town was about 800 people and the base several thousand.

Strangely enough, a man that had known my Father owned the Hardware store. I remember a set of dishes we bought and used for years. It was two sets that had been damaged. The pattern and style were the same but were a breakfast and a dinner set. We had 12 or 14 of everything.

We bought our first car there. We needed something fast with the baby coming. We found a Ford Coupe, probably out of the 30s. It didn't last well; in fact it was a wreck. We bought a Sedan and had that when David arrived in May.

Life got a little hectic. President Roosevelt died in April, David was born May 21, R. G. had his 23 birthday May 31.

I went to the Hospital Friday night and David was born Monday night. R. G. was Officer of the Day and the first 300 German Prisoners were moved in the Night David was born. R G spent the time running back and forth seeing how I was doing and getting the prisoners settled.

After 52 hours I had a baby. The baby wasn't doing well, I was fine and RG was a wreck.

The Germans were Rommel's Panzer troops from North Africa. A lot of them were Engineers. The stockade was on one side of the flagpole, the library on the next corner, Headquarters on the third and the Post office on the fourth.

The wives coming and going could be seen from the Stockade. There was a lot of whistling and yelling until someone explained to the Germans that these were not ladies of questionable repute, these were wives of the personnel. Women in 1945 wore bright red lipstick. German women that wore red lipstick were prostitutes.

The POWs were locked up but no one worried if they got out. It was 50 miles through the desert to the next town. It didn't take long to send up a fighter plane and bring them back. The POWs were put on work detail. They insisted that only one man in each group spoke English. They would read the papers to each other and the papers were in English.

R. G was a brand new 2nd Lt. He had a Photo Lab to run. The first WAFs he had worked with were assigned to the photo lab. It was a new experience especially since his training was in Aerial Photo.

He had received equipment to develop film from aerial cameras. The machine was about twelve feet long and three feet long. They had to be installed inside concrete curbs about 6 inches tall. The G. I.s had worked all morning trying to get the machines over the curb. The German POWs were sent to help. One of the older men finally had enough. He asked R. G. if he could have his men do the job. Being Engineers they knew exactly how to do it. It was done in about ten minutes.

About a month after David's birth we got a phone call from my Father. No one had phones so R. G. had to come get me, take me to the phone office in town and call him back. He had just returned from Europe. He made the D-Day Landing. He was almost too old to be in the service but since he had no dependants, he volunteered for the Army. I was never sure why he called after all those years.

In July we saw the light from the first A-bomb test in Almagordo. We thought it was a lightning storm. Nothing was mentioned in the news. It was about 60 miles away so light was most of what we saw.

Years later when David's fingers and toes clubbed my theory was the radiation. The Medics in Bethesda and Ft Belvoir would go along with that if it had been before instead of after he was born. They could never come up with anything except idiopathic clubbing. Fallout of the radiation did fog the first sheet of film in every film pack in the lab. They also proved in later years that more babies born in that area had heart defects than the average population.

1945 was a little scrambled. RG graduated from Cadets and became a 2nd Lt. in February. We left immediately for Ft Sumner, N M. We rented a small apartment between the town and the Base. It had a large living room, a bedroom and a kitchen.

President Roosevelt died in April of that year.

David was born at the Base Hospital on May 21, 1945.

RG had his 23rd birthday on May 31. I had my 19th birthday on June 22. The first A bomb blast was at Alamogordo, NM about the middle of July. We saw the light, since it was only 60 miles away. We didn't know for months what we had seen since there was no news that might aid the enemy. The War in Japan was over in August and the War in Europe ended in May.

RG had been sent to California to be shipped to Japan when the Japanese surrendered. I had taken David and gone to Olton and was staying with his parents.

RG was reassigned to Riverside, Ca and came home to get David and me. I remember driving to Clovis, the nearest he could get by train, to pick him up. His father was driving, the sand was blowing so hard you couldn't see the front end of the car.

Riverside, CA

We packed the baby and all our worldly goods in the car and drove to R. G.'s new assignment in Riverside. The Air Base was at the base of a hill. There were warning red lights on top of the hill. Many a pilot mistook them for the lights of another plane and slid down the other side of the hill in a crash landing.

We made trips to Lake Arrowhead and Big Bear Lake while we were there. Dave Kolic was stationed there a few weeks and met his namesake.

We were not in Riverside many months when the Military started discharging the men. So back to Civilian life!

We moved to Lubbock. We had a tiny apartment on North H street until we got an apartment at Lubbock Air Force Base. The base had been closed and the barracks cut into two room apartments.

While we lived on Ave. H Robert was born at Lubbock Hospital. RG had gotten a job in Public Relations at South Plains Army AirField. With two babies we had to have more room and moved to what is now Reese AFB on the other side of Lubbock.

Fort Sam Houston, TX

Robert was just a few months old when a job in San Antonio became available. This job was at Ft Sam Houston and RG was editing the Fourth Arm Recruiter.

The first place we lived was the drawing room of an old mansion. Ft Sam had been there since the Indian Wars and a lot of the Generals had retired in that area. There were many large homes that had been cut up into apartments. There were a few elderly senior officers living in big homes but most of them had been cut up to help the housing shortage.

We later moved a few blocks away to a little house behind another large home. This was the servants quarters and had a large bedroom, a living room-dining room, kitchen and bath.

I always loved San Antonio. You could almost see history. Eisenhour was a young officer there. He met Mamie and married her there. Their first home was in base housing and they were living there when they lost their first son.

The parade ground is MacArthur Field but Arthur not Douglas. Wainwright came back from POW camp in Japan while we were there. Indirectly he helped us with transportation when we went to Trinidad .

We used to take the kids to the zoo at Brackenridge Park. I really think it was for our amusement, not the children. We would go down to the Riverwalk and eat tamales that we had bought at Woolworth's. We made several visits to the Alamo. It had not been restored then as it is now. We used to drive to the old Missions that are around San Antonio.

One Sunday morning R. G. and the boys walked around the block to the Post Office. To his surprise, he received a notice from the Air Force that he had been recalled and would report immediately. The letter said that R. G. would be in the US for at least a year. They recalled him as a Tank Officer and that should have given us a clue. At that time the Air Force had no tanks.

The part about staying in the US was not true either. Three weeks later he was in Panama! He was there a few weeks and transferred to Trinidad. He joined a unit that was mapping South America. We couldn't join him until quarters were available. Since Waller is in the center of the Island and there are a limited number of family quarters, we had to wait until someone was sent back to the States.

When we finally got orders to join him we had to depend on the Army which was a block away to take care or Air Force transportation. It was almost impossible for several weeks and suddenly they couldn't be more co-operative. I didn't find out for years what had happened.

Having no car, we walked everywhere. The boys were 18 months and 3. About two doors from the Post Office was a small liquor store. Robert loved to stop and talk to the man that owned it. He would stay for the few minutes it took me to go to the post office and pick up the mail. I mentioned the problems we were having with the Military. Wainwright was a customer of Mr. Albert's and by this time Wainwright was the Commanding General. Mr. Albert mentioned our problem and Wainwright told the Red Cross Director to see what could be done. We went from "It can't be done" to " can we send a car or pick up your tickets for you?"

We had gone through San Antonio about 5 years later and were talking to some of the people in the area. Mr. Albert was dead by then and so was Wainwright but someone remembered how they had stepped in and helped. I always wished I could have told them how much it meant to me.

More than 50 years later it is funny, then it wasn't. At that time a woman had problems signing any papers or contracts on her own. She had to be 21 to do that. I was 20 and had the two boys. The bank had RG's power of Attorney and I'm sure cut some corners to help me.

Then came the fun part. I applied for my passport and had to have a certified copy of my Birth Certificate. I got it. I had no given name, just baby Savage. There was a family discussion when I was born about my name. Since something had to be filed they were told to file the certificate and send an amendment later. The Birth Certificate got to Austin. The Amendment went in and before it was forwarded the courthouse was burned. All records went with it. Not knowing this, I had never had to have a copy before, it was never corrected.

I was told they would issue the Passport since I was traveling on Government Orders but to get the Birth Certificate corrected when I got back. It took 5 years. I would get an affidavit from my Grandparents that they were present when I was born and knew the circumstances. It would be notarized and sent in. I would get it back that it wasn't sufficient. I finally told them to forget it and send me a true copy of what they had. I guess they figured they had gone and far as they could, the   corrected it and sent me a copy. I have a birth certificate about 3 feet long now, but I have one.

I have often wondered if I would have nerve enough to start on the trip to Trinidad if I hadn't been young and naïve. It never crossed my mind that it was a problem or that I wouldn't go.

We left San Antonio on the train and went to New Orleans. There we were taken to Lake Ponchitrain and quartered for a few days. We were loaded aboard the "Private Thomas" and sailed late in the afternoon. I had pictured New Orleans as being on the Gulf of Mexico. We didn't get to the Gulf until about Midnight. Hitting rough water in the middle of the night was startling.

We shared a cabin with another wife and her son. We had one of the two cabins on board with a private bath. Most of the passengers were below the water line in open bays. Since there were only two cabins on board and a Col. and his family had the other, I have wondered how we were so lucky.

The Thomas was a MATS ship. It had a round keel instead of a traditional one. We noticed this when we hit a hurricane in the Gulf. The Mess Hall was in the center of the ship and had windows on either side. I will never forget sitting there for meals. One child was in a chair, the other in a high chair. I had to keep my foot on the high chair to keep it from sliding when the ship rolled.

The ship would roll from side to side and you could see the horizon first on one side, then the other. Then it would roll The other way and you could hear the propellers come out of the water and roar. I can't imagine why we didn't get seasick. I guess we didn't have time.

Then we arrived in Panama and the band was on the dock playing. Someone ran out and said Welcome to Panama. We were there two or three days. The Wives that were returning to the States gave us a good inspection. The were in knee length dresses and ours were the new ankle length.

We left Panama and sailed to Puerto Rico. Again the band played and the bus from Ramey met us and took us to the AFBase to wait for a plane to take us to Trinidad. We were there about a week because Waller AFB had been told the ship was late and it was actually early.

One of the crews from Waller came in for supplies. They agreed to put the bucket seats back in and we left for Trinidad.

There were seven women and we had 5 children with us. It was impossible to tighten the seat belts enough to keep the kids on the seats. We couldn't get sweaters when it got cold because the luggage was in cargo nets. We had been told to bring food because it was about 8 hours flight and we were on our own to feed the kids.

We had gone to the snack bar and Bacon, lettuce and tomato sandwiches were the only thing we could find that looked like they would pack for that long. The bacon was half cooked and the bread was about an inch thick. It was years before I had a BLT again.

We arrived at Waller about Midnight in a driving rain. We got off the plane and ran for the Hanger. The OD looked up and said, "Where in the Hell did you come from?" The urge was to climb back on the plane.

Our sponsors had not been informed since our trip was not scheduled. There was a USO show that night and nearly everyone had gone. We had no idea where our quarters were.

RG finally showed up. He had heard the plane come in and said he had a feeling we were on it.

Bobby would have nothing to do with his father. He talked about his other father! At 18 months he could not believe the Daddy in San Antonio was the Daddy in Trinidad.

I guess that would have gone on but the furniture arrived and I had shipped a Motor Scooter. Since Bobby wanted to ride the scooter it broke the ice with his father.

We had two seasons in Trinidad.   In the Dry season it rained a couple of times a day. In the Rainy season it rained all day every day. Most of us didn't have cars so you got where you were going dripping wet. Everyone was wet so you really didn't notice.

The houses were on stilts 8 feet off the ground. There was a concrete slab under the house and the washer and dryer were there. There were no glass windows. The windows had wooden louvers. The gardeners had to keep the vines cut back or they came up the stairs and through the windows.

We had assorted snakes. Boas were a problem. Night watchmen were posted at night. Their job was to watch for snakes. The week we arrived a 14 foot Boa was found under the Kindergarten.

The compound was cleared of vegetation. The jungle surrounded it and was full of parrots. Sunrise and hundreds of parrots makes alarm clocks unnecessary.

Waller was in the middle of an island about 45 miles square. Port of Spain is the capital. Your first trip to town was something to remember. Few people had cars so you took the native bus. As you come into town you notice the houses have outside showers. The shower openings are toward the street. There are no shower curtains.

Children don't wear pants or bottoms to their clothes until they are about 4. No wet pants, they go where it is convenient.

The first person you see go to the middle of the street and dump the garbage is startling. Not nearly as starting as the Vultures that swoop down and eat the garbage. They do a good job.

English is the official language. The people are black, oriental or white. All have a British accent. The British are usually remittance men. They were usually from affluent families that wanted to get an embarrassment out of England. The family sent money as long as the family member stayed away from England

The Orientals were usually Chinese that were sent in as slave labor to work in the early days. They, too, have lived in Trinidad for generations.

There is an Indian Influence in the food. It was the first time I had ever had my Thanksgiving Turkey Curried.

Everyone was so pleased that they could afford a maid.   I tried but found it more trouble than it was worth. I was aware of the disease on the Island. Average life expectancy was 36 years. I refused to let the maids touch the children or their food. I was the only one on Waller that didn't have to have children treated for internal parasites.

The main road ran between the housing area and the base proper. The natives walked through the base but had to stay on the road. The first time you saw Elephantiasis or leprosy was a jolt. TB was one of the killers and so many people were infected. Americans were returned to the US immediately if they tested positive. I always thought that was a little late, but they didn't ask me.

The Base had been huge in WW2. A large part of it had been deserted. Rows of Barracks and other military building were being destroyed by nature. The vines would climb the buildings and pull them to pieces. The first time I saw this was on a ride on the motor scooter. The orchids grew wild and RG told me how to get to one tree that was covered in tiny red orchids. It was about 60 feet tall with orchids all the way down.

Most of the Americans grew orchids on old boards under their quarters. Since you had a place the size of your house under your house there was plenty of room. I never managed to get them to grow. But then, I can't grow anything anywhere.

We were in Trinidad in 1948-49. From Port of Spain you could see across the water to Venezuela. The Bay was filled with hundreds of masts of sunken ships. The Ships came to Venezuela during the war to load Oil. Since it is just 7 miles the troops would shoot the ships from Port of Spain. Of course, anything coming into Port of Spain Harbor was sunk with fire from Venezuela. The ships were just dragged out of the channel and left to rust. It was years after the war before they were removed.

We had a Hospital on Waller. Sort of a dispensary that cured everything with rubbing alcohol or methialate. As soon as we arrived and saw the problem I had my grandfather send what children needed for day to day living. Peroxide, bandages, talcum, calamine and the bare essentials. We were better supplied than the Hospital. He sent a package a month and we used them all.

David had broken his collarbone in San Antonio. It had healed but was still tender on the boat trip. The Hurricane threw him out of the bunk onto the deck. He was screaming and I was afraid he had broken it again. He hadn't but our first stop the day we got to Waller was the Hospital. That is when we learned how well supplied they were. We seemed to live through it.

We joined the Squadron in Trinidad but the rest of the people had been in Panama for some years and moved to Trinidad. The mapping job that they had been doing was about over so we were sent back to the states.

We were sent back on a ship that had been stopped on its way back from South America and all the wives, children, animals, furniture and vehicles loaded on. The ship had been transferring displaced persons from Europe to South America. It had not been cleaned before we were loaded aboard. It was not surprising that we went to the hospital in New York when we landed.

We had a few officers on Board but most of them were flown back to the States. The Aircraft had to be ferried back. We were to go to Mountain Home, Idaho. We had a change of orders on the way and went to Ft Dix, NJ. With the usual efficiency, most of the furniture and equipment and animals went to Mountain Home.

Picture Trinidad, seven degrees north of the Equator. It is February. The ship took us from the tropics to New York Harbor in February. There were no winter clothes in Trinidad. The Fathers went shopping when the got to NYC since they were several days ahead of the ship. Fathers do not know about fitting children's clothing and nothing fit. We finally ended up dumping everything in a pile and finding things that would do until we could shop.

David had gotten sick on the boat and by the time we arrived I was sick. RG had come ahead and he was sick, too. We all ended up in Ft Hamilton's Hospital. RG was assured that the paperwork would be handled by the Hospital. It was the first time he was AWOL. The Squadron had no idea what had happened to us for ten days.

David went into the Hospital the day we arrived. R. G. and I got sick a few days later and Bobby was put in the same ward as David as a boarder. The nurse said they would put them in adjoining cribs. When we came to pick them up ten days later they were at opposite ends of the Ward.

Bobby tired of Hospital Routine. He wasn't ill and was not happy confined to bed. Each morning a urine specimen was collected from each child. Bobby altered the routine and poured his morning Pineapple juice directly into the specimen cup.

The nurse said it wasn't long before the Dr and the Lab Tech showed up. They said they had never tested a specimen with that high a sugar content. Bobby admitted what he had done.

R. G. said it must have been shortly after that when the Dr. showed up at his Ward to inform him of the problem.

I think the Ward heaved a sigh of relief when they returned our children to our care.

McGuire, N. J.

We arrived in Mount Holly, N. J. and our first place was a two room apt. It had a large bedroom and a small kitchen. We survived there for a few weeks and rented a house in Vincentown. It was an old farmhouse that had been moved into the little town. The front door opened almost in the street but the back yard was huge. A bathroom had been installed when we moved in and the old outhouse was removed.

The house had a large kitchen, small dining room and small living room on the first floor. On the second floor were three bedrooms and a large bath. The Bath had been a bedroom and was turned into a bath. The third floor was a full attic that was unfinished. It made a great place to hang clothes when it rained.

New Jersey has beautiful topsoil and is known for its vegetables. Not to be out done, when spring came we planted. It didn't take long to realize that we had flunked farming. The topsoil was about 18 inches of topsoil over harder subsoil.

We got onion sets and RG hit on the idea of taking a broomstick and making holes and dropping the sets in. They did beautifully. We had the longest, thinnest onions ever seen. Tasted fine.

We branched out into black-eyed peas. Black-eyed peas were unknown to the local population and they had no idea of how to prepare them. The peas did grow and multiply. One of the neighbors said they tried everything and finally ate them with catsup. No one thought to tell them about the Southern custom of cooking everything with ham or bacon.

The cucumbers and carrots did fine.

Ft Dix even set aside land and let those that lived on base have plots for gardens. Ft Dix was the Army post that joined McGuire.

In the time we were in New Jersey we made trips to Barnagot lighthouse and several trips to the beaches.

R. G. had a Base Photo Lab. All the Photo equipment sent back from Trinidad was sent to the Lab. This included 125 Speed Graphics that were hard to account for. Our government had given the cameras to South American Countries. The military had no use for them and would leave them lying around. Our G Is resented the free gifts to unappreciative Countries. Therefore, they liberated them and brought them back to Trinidad. R. G. Finally turned them in as Found On Post. I have often wondered what the Pentagon made of that report!

Next came orders for Barksdale, La.

Barksdale, La.

Barksdale is in Shreveport, La. We were delighted because we were near Texas. Or course, we were still 500 miles from home but that is not an impossible trip.

We found a duplex in a civilian housing area adjacent to the Base. It was two stories. Living room and kitchen on the first floor and two bedrooms and bath on the second. Or neighbors in the one floor duplex next door were the Comptroller and his family. They had recently returned from a tour in Germany. They had three children and had brought their German maid and her five-year-old son back with them. With the aid of the Catholic association Yada and her son had gotten a visa for them to immigrate to this Country.

This probably wouldn't have stuck in my memory but Yada had been in a concentration camp. She was one of the few survivors. She was in her 20s and had a good command of the English language by this time. I have often wondered what happened to them.

Some time later we moved to one on the next street but it was similar to the first. Our neighbors here were another member of the Photo Squadron that R. G. was in.   He was OD one night and a top secret experimental delta wing plane made an unscheduled landing. The papers the next morning carried a story of the Lubbock lights that had been spotted across the southwest. I don't think I ever worried about people from another planet after that. When someone you know has seen a UFO and talked to the crew it is not strange any more.

I learned another lesson at Barksdale that has lasted me the rest of my life. The order came out that there would be intergration of the troops and the formerly all white outfits would have some blacks assigned. Being an outfit composed of Southerners, there was some concern about friction. We were called into a lecture and told there would be no incidents. We were free to think what we liked but we would act as we were told.

The first black person sent in was a Captain. He was a pilot named Newsome. He was a bachelor and arrived by himself. He was assigned quarters in the BOQ and ate at the Officer's Mess. There was heard muttering that he couldn't eat at their table. He made no attempt to. He was polite but distant. Next you heard that no one would fly with him. Then they found out he was a four engine pilot that didn't make mistakes. It wasn't long until men were fighting to get on his crew.

Some of the Enlisted Blacks were sent in and there was no trouble. Given a chance, the whites learned to know them as fellow military men instead of by their color.

It was a lesson I have never forgotten. It sounds impossible but I can remember what a person looks like but cannot remember color. Color just does not register in my brain.

While we were stationed there the Air Force was made a separate branch of the service. It had been the Army Air Force up to that time. The main thing I noticed was that the cannon was not fired at sunset. The Uniform stayed the same for awhile before it was changed to Air Force Blue. It is funny the things you remember.

are   # MacDill AFB, FL

The summer of 1950 we were transferred to MacDill. We got there in July and David started First Grade in September.

When we got to Tampa and rented a house. A GI had bought the house and had gotten transferred before he could move in. We moved in and in October the Contractor that built the house showed up. He wanted to know why we were living in his house. The Loan for the GI had fallen through. He had turned the house over to a realtor and we were paying rent to a person that didn't own the house.

The Legal Officer advised R. G. that we could remain since we had rented in good faith. We decided that the best thing would be to buy the house. We signed the papers on the 28th of Dec 1950 so we could homestead the house for the next year.

The Lawyer handling the sale for us was Gibbons. He was later a member of the House of Representatives for more than 40 years. His wife was the Notary.

The house cost $6,800 and the interest rate was 4%!! Last year a house in the next block sold for $104,000 and I can only imagine what the interest rate was. Forty-nine years has made a big difference in the cost of real estate.

R. G. took over the Base Photo Lab. He was also Squadron Adjutant and a few other things. The one that was the most amusing took years to figure out. He was called in and briefed on a job. He was issued his Identification card and it was locked with his orders in the Base Safe. He said he was confused at the time but later found out that he had been assigned the task of going to the proper base, picking up the detonator for the Atomic Bomb and escorting it to the designated place. Luckily, he never had to do this.

Robert started school in 1951 in Port Tampa. David was in second grade there by then.

R. G. was gone to school, TDY or something else most of the three years we were in Tampa.

David would always tell his Father that he and Bobby had nothing to eat but sandwiches and TV dinners all the time he was gone. To my knowledge, they had neither. It was enough to get sympathy from their Father until he learned the truth.

Manhattan School opened in 1953 and both boys were transferred to Manhattan.

R. G. had been transferred to West Drayton, Middlesex, England in late 1954. As soon as quarters were available we moved again.

Overseas moves are more interesting than local moves. You have to separate your worldly possessions into hand luggage, hold baggage, household goods to accompany you and household goods for storage. I can guarantee you that things don't always go where they should.

With our usual good planning, we went from Tampa to England in January. I can assure you England was much colder. In fact, England is always cold and damp.

We drove from Tampa to Charlottesville, VA and spent a couple of weeks with my Aunt Barbara and her family. There is usually a delay from the time your household goods are picked up and the date of your transportation overseas. We visited Barbara and Ed and the boys went to school with Ellen for a couple of weeks.

It was cold and snowy in Charlottesville but we were able to do some sightseeing. We took the children to Luray Caverns in the mountains west of Charlottesville. Barbara and I did a lot of sewing, including a winter coat for me.

One of the oldest woolen mills in the country was in Charlottesville. They put the yardage that they didn't need to fill an order on sale at the mill. We bought some beautiful gray wool and Barbara cheered me on while I sewed. When we got through I told her that I wouldn't have had the nerve to try making a coat if she hadn't been there to show me how. Her reply was that she had never done anything like this but wanted to see if I could. I wore that coat for years.

We toured Monticello while we were there. A hurricane had gone through this area in the past year and a lot of the huge old trees were down. The house was not damaged.

Since Ed was Dean of History at University of Virginia they had spent a lot of time at Monticello. In fact, at that time one of the clubs had an annual dinner there. I can imagine what it must have been like by candlelight.

We drove on to Ft Hamilton, NY in Brooklyn and delivered the car to the Brooklyn Naval Yard for shipment. It was snowing just to make things more difficult. We were quartered in the old Barracks on Ft Hamilton for a few days and then boarded ship. We were some of the last to use the barracks. They were old and there was a lot of concern about fire with that many women and children staying there.

Our stay was uneventful. We didn't have time to sightsee and in the cold it wouldn't have been much fun.

West Drayton, Middlesex, England

We arrived in South Hampton after a week aboard a MATS ship. We chose that instead of a large commercial ship. We docked in South Hampton and R. G. had rented a car and met us.

The drive back was amusing. He handed me the road map to navigate. I was used to between 10 and 50 miles to the inch on a map. These were an inch to a mile. We missed a lot of checkpoints.

Our first meal in England was on the way to London. We stopped at a roadside Pub and had a mixed grill. I think it must have been the best meal we had in England. English food leaves something to be desired.

Our first apartment was in Drayton Gardens, West Drayton, Middlesex, England. The name was bigger than the Apartment. It was the end apartment on the upstairs of a six apartment building.

R. G. had hired the lady that had the downstairs apartment to get the place ready for us. The Hold baggage had arrived. I had sent linens, dishes and pots and pans. She had never seen a fitted sheet and the first night was interesting with sheets that had not been tucked in.

A lot of funny things happened as I got to know the Stammers. That was the name of the lady downstairs and her husband. They had both been raised in North London.

Most of the offices and businesses that an American had to go to were around Piccadilly Circus. The Ladies of the Evening also plied their trade around Piccadilly Circus. An American GI was easy to spot even in civilian clothes. They wore their hair much shorter than any Englishman would. The Ladies took great delight in making a play for the GI especially if his wife accompanied him.

Mrs. Stammers thought this was very funny. Then she and her husband were around Piccadilly Circus one night. She was holding her husband's arm when the Lady made her pitch. She was livid. After that when the subject came up she did not see it as amusing.

The lady's husband instructed me in the fine art of building a fire in the fireplace and keeping the water heater in the kitchen going. The one in the Kitchen had a water jacket around a coke fire. It is not easy to make a fire with coke. Coke is baked or processed coal and takes a much hotter fire to get it started. Kindling just won't do it. At least, it wouldn't do it for me. He tried to show me how to empty the ashes and start a fire. Finally in desperation he had a gas poker made that I could run from the Cooking stove to the Coke fire. Then all I had to do was put the poker in the coke and let it get hot enough to burn.

The hot water from the coke stove went into an overhead tank in the top of the hall closet. This kept the dampness out and the linens dry.

One of my first lessons was I did not speak the English language. After a few embarrassing mistakes I learned to describe my needs to and English Lady next door and then go shopping armed with the proper word or phrase.

I also found it confusing that some things were sold at strange places. I never did figure out why you bought soap at the Hardware store.

We spent the winter months going to indoor places like Museums and famous buildings. In the summer we went to outdoor places. London Zoo was a favorite and Whipsnade was another. Whipsnade is the country home for the Zoo. It is about 30 miles north of London in the rural countryside. A lot of the animals in Whipsnade run loose and the people are fenced in.

Some of the fruit and vegetables you buy in England are not to the American taste. Some of the Oranges come from the Canary Islands and are bitter to our taste. The Monkeys at London Zoo love them and at that time you were welcome to feed the animals. The Monkeys would scream and jump up and down when they saw anyone carrying a paper bag. I have wondered if feeding the animals started during the War when food was rationed and it must have been hard to feed the animals. The War had been over just a few years when we lived there.

Candy came off rationing about the time we arrived. The British have a sweet tooth so this was welcome news.

We were forbidden to eat bread off the economy. Our flour was sent to the local bakeries and bread was made for the commissary. The British flour was not approved for us to eat.   Since Elevenses and Tea at 4 PM consists of sandwiches and cake most of us ate the local bread. It didn't seem to harm us. The Teacakes and Petit Fours were wonderful.

We did have a problem with the vegetables. Most Vegetables are imported. Beets, Broccoli and Brussel Sprouts are grown in England. Good potatoes are grown and the best strawberries I have ever eaten. Every Englishman that can get a tiny plot of land has a garden. We had a very small garden at the first apartment we had. Since we were not interested in a garden we let our downstairs neighbor use it. The second house had a large garden and we did use that one. Potatoes had been planted the year before and we were still harvesting them. There were ever bearing strawberries in the flowerbed. Six plants kept us supplied in fruit.

Another American couple lived a few doors away. They were interested in trying American Vegetables since we were told that several things wouldn't grow. The growing season is very short. One of these vegetables was Iceberg lettuce. The other couple started lettuce plants in flats indoors and gave us some when it was time to transplant. They were right. The lettuce would look fine and about the time it should mature it would shoot up in one long stalk. We never did get it to make a head.

Another problem we had with fresh Vegetables was the lack of Minerals in the soil. The land has been used constantly for so long that the Vegetables lack minerals.

By the time we had been there three years we looked like we had sunburn that didn't go within about an inch of our hairline. We were given Supplemental Vitamins and Minerals that did little good. We were told we would be all right when we got back to the States and on a regular diet. By the time you were back in the States six months it was gone.

I have read stories in the Computer about modern England. When we lived in West Drayton it was a small town. It had been there a long time. Cromwell was chasing the King trying to capture him. He thought the King was hiding in the local church. At that time a Church was a whole town. There were still bullet holes in the Church gates that Cromwell's men put there.

Part of the old Church wall was in the back yard of our first apartment. British law says you can't tear down something like that but neither do you have to repair it. Give enough centuries it will disappear. Since it is sold brick about eight bricks thick it takes time. Our apartment house was where the Church blacksmith had been. The big metal rings for tying the horse when he was shod were still in our little garden. Around the corner was a grocery. It had been the jail.

The Travel Advertisements list a Supermarket on that spot. Since it is about ten feet square and there was no way of enlarging it since the wall was behind it I would like to see that.

When we were there the only Hotel in West Drayton was a house on the green that was very old and had about five bedrooms. I read now that there is a 465-room hotel with ballroom, meeting rooms and an indoor swimming pool where the old pub on Cherry Lane used to be. There is also another 350-room hotel on the main road across from Heathrow.

The old Roman Road was between Heathrow and West Drayton. Now there is an up and over major highway. I think I would rather remember it the way it was when I was there.

The boys went to Bushy Park to school. The bus picked them up at the NCO club on base in the morning and dropped them off in the evening. Most of the year it was dark at 8 AM when they were picked up and dark again at 3 PM when they returned.

To get to Bushy the bus had to go around Heathrow. On English roads it can be confusing. One afternoon the bus was late. As time went on we became more panicky. The Police didn't have a report of an accident but by the time the bus was three hours over due we were worried. It finally arrived. The bus had a new driver that day and he got lost. The children kept trying to tell him he was on the wrong road but he wouldn't believe them.

We have often wondered about the effects of places on people. The School building at Bushy Park was the Headquarters for Eisenhower in WW2. The Second grade was in his old office. The plans for the D-Day invasion were made there. Their High School in Japan was the Kamikaze school for the Japanese Suicide Pilots. Does the Vibes of the Past linger and effect the people of the future?

The British were at War with the Irish and had been for years. It got a little worse and the word got out that they were going to make a raid on West Drayton RAF Station to get arms. The Americans shared the Base with the RAF.

I was going to the Commissary one morning. To get to the Base you turned off the main Road, went down about a block and made a sharp right turn into the Base. I turned the corner that morning and found myself staring at the business end of the largest gun I ever saw. It was mounted on a Tank and aimed at incoming traffic. That was almost fifty years ago and the British and Irish are still fighting.

One of the first things you learn when you drive a car in England is that they drive on the other, to Americans the wrong, side of the road. The only time I had trouble was when I was driving alone and there were no other cars. I soon learned which side was mine.

Americans are given a driver's license for a year before they have to take the driver's test. I don't know why. Most Americans find it easier to leave the country for a few days and get a fresh stamp on their passport. That gives them another year without the test. The Military were in and out often enough it didn't bother them but most of the wives took a trip.

Mine was to Holland. The boys were in school and R. G. didn't have time off so I went alone. R. G.s housekeeping was different but no one starved or froze. I never did figure out why he washed wool GI blankets with the rest of the washing. It was itchy for awhile but no harm done.

I was three weeks late for the tulip season but so were the tulips that year. We had a cold spring so I got there when everything was in full bloom. The weather was sunny and cold. Since it was an Air Force sponsored trip we had guides and reservations made ahead.

You can't imagine how beautiful the fields of tulips were unless you saw them. Each morning the farmers cut the blossoms off the tulips. This was supposed to make the bulbs grow better. They used the tulip heads to decorate their yards, wagons or anything else that appealed to them. We also went to a park that was made to show off the different kinds and colors of tulips.

One Art Museum had a number of Rembrant paintings. I had always imagined his pictures as 8 x 10 or 11x 16. One covered the entire wall.

The Dutch food is wonderful and the country is so clean you could eat off the sidewalk in safety. The Dutch housewife cleans the house and scrubs the front step and sidewalk every morning. The front step is white marble and is always shining.

The food shows the influence of many other countries. Dutch chocolate and pastries are some of the best I have ever tasted.

Most of the Dutch use bicycles instead of cars. Seldom a night goes by that someone doesn't park his car and let it roll into the canal. Since the canal is deep and the wall straight down, getting the car out is a job.

The canals are opened every night and fresh seawater is washed through them. Transportation for most people is either a boat or a streetcar. The streetcars are sometimes several cars long and on the back of the last car is a mailbox. Mail is put in all the way along the route and when the car gets to the Post Office it is emptied. Your mail is in the main Post Office within a few minutes of mailing.

We went to Scotland for our vacation. It was July but everyone told us to take warm clothes. That was a summer that had almost no rain. Instead of the constant gray skies, we had Sunshine. By the time we got to northern Scotland the sun set about 11:30 PM and was up and shining bright at 2 AM. We had already had a taste of winter sun in London. The children left for school at 9 A M in darkness and got home at 3:30 PM in total darkness.

Our idea was to drive up the eastern side of England and Scotland and back down the Western side. It didn't take us long to learn several important lessons. The first was that you eat at mealtime or you don't eat. This was before the days of Fast Food in England. You also have to book ahead. Since we never knew where we would be at any specific time this was impossible. We did have a car full of snack food and we did a lot of snacking.

We found a beautiful Inn near a lake. As usual we didn't have a reservation but they found us a room on the third floor. We thought it might have been one of the maid's but we were delighted. That was when we noticed that the sun didn't go down at a reasonable time. The boys insisted it couldn't be bedtime.

These Inns were vacation places that most people spent a week or two in. If you planned on hiking the next day you informed the Waiter the night before. He had a lunch packed for you for the next day. We were sorry we didn't have the time to spend a few days and hike through the countryside.

We were even able to see Balmoral; the Queens summer residence, in the distance. Since it is in a wooded area and no one is allowed near we were lucky. A storm the winter before had blown a number of huge trees down and Balmoral was visible from the road.

One of the things that stands out in my mind was the night we spent in Edinborough. We wanted to go there since my great grandparents had come from there.

We spent the night in the Inn that Stevenson used as the setting for "Kidnapped." We had a very large cat that spent the night with us. I guess it was the cat's room.

R. G. always said that if you are in a strange place and don't know about their food, order fried eggs. No one can ruin a fried egg. His breakfast eggs were fried in Mutton Fat. Sort of reminds you of candle wax! He realized that if you try hard enough you could ruin a fried Egg.

A lot of the roads in Northern Scotland were one lane. There were lay-bys or pull off places every half mile or so. If you met another car, one of you had to back to the nearest lay-by. Remember this was not on flat land. The hills weren't steep but driving backwards was an adventure.

Each field is fenced with stone. No mortar just stacked stones. The farmer picks up any stone he sees as he crosses the field and stacks it in the fence. After hundreds of years the fences are sizable. They are also absolutely straight. Some go right up the hill and look like they were laid out with a ruler.

We were somewhere in the Highlands and there was nothing in sight as far as you could see. We heard a bagpipe somewhere in the distance. It was the one of the most beautiful thing I ever heard.

Early on a Sunday morning we were on the main road and heard a bagpipe in the distance. It was a Piper playing while a group of young schoolboys marched down the road. We thought they might have been going to church.

One of the saddest and most beautiful things we saw was a Church. In the days when Bonny Prince Charlie was fighting the English a lot of fighting and destroying was done in Scotland. The Church was more a Cathedral. I had burned and only the walls were standing. We got out of the car to look at it and were amazed. It looked like it was carpeted in green. The grass had grown and a perfect cover. You could only imagine what it must have been with stain-glass windows and heavy doors.

At the Scotland-England border a lot of sheep run loose. People pull off the road where they can look at both countries. The sheep have found out that they can beg food. Even though they wear yokes to keep them from getting through the fence, they manage to go where the cars are. Since we were entering England we figured we would eat lunch somewhere and be home that night. We fed the sheep every bite we had left in the car.

It was Sunday and we started looking for a place to eat. The Hotels had to have reservations. We finally found a small café that looked a little run down but by this time we were desperate. We ordered sandwiches to go. While we were waiting we watched a swarm of flies. A large swarm was flying in a large circle. We left with our sandwiches and fed them to the first dog we saw. I wouldn't have been able to gag one down and I knew I wasn't going to let the children eat them.

We found an ice cream vender in one of the towns along the way and that was all we had to eat until we arrived in London and our Apartment.

Our trip back to the USA was a little of everything. We got to Preswick Scotland on the first leg of our trip. We were to catch a plane there for the trip home. Something was delayed and we spent about 5 days there. There was not much to do, cars had been sent on, we were quartered on a military base. We spent a lot of time sitting and talking.

The day finally arrived and we left Preswick. The plane went to Shannon, Ireland. We had a few hours layover while we were refueled. This gave us time to try to buy out the Gift shop.

All my life I had heard about the Emerald Isle. I saw with my own eyes what they were talking about. From the air the land is the most beautiful shade of green I have ever seen.

We left Shannon and flew to New York City. We had an uneventful flight. When we landed we found out that a plane an hour ahead of us on the same route had crashed and lost all on board. This is a sobering idea.

The plane was a group of Canadian War Brides from England. They had chartered a plane and gone to England for a visit. The excuse was given as bad weather but we certainly had no bad weather. It makes you rethink how sudden death may come.

We arrived at Idlewild and picked up the car. We drove to Springfield, Mass and rented a house. We borrowed army cots from Westover.

Several days later we drove back to Idlewild to pick up Sam, the Siamese cat. We had checked him in at the RSPCA at Heathrow a couple of weeks before. We didn't have to ask if the cat had arrived. You could hear the complaints he was making before we got out of the car.

We drove back to Springfield with a very irate cat in his carrying case in the back of the car.

Westover, Mass.

I spent three years in England dreaming of getting back to the states and warm dry weather. England was gray and foggy and rainy. I wore fur boots most of the year and carried an umbrella all the time. I couldn't wait to get back to sunshine and dry weather.

In Springfield summer was on a Thursday that year. We got home in July and it was blanket weather. This is with our GI cots and no furniture.

I had never put up storm windows before but I learned.

We would have snow and before you got the sidewalks shoveled, it snowed again. The law required you to clean the sidewalks within in a few hours of the snow. Then the snow plows came down the street and piled the snow across the driveway. England was better!

Springfield and Chicopee Falls were close to Westover. A lot of military families lived in these towns.

The scenery was wonderful on a good day. When the apple trees were turning red in the fall it was beautiful. From the top of the hills you could look down on miles of red and yellow leaves.

You could also buy fresh apple cider on the roadside. The first few days in the refrigerator it was nice, the next few days it was a little nippy. After that it would blow the cork out of the bottle when you opened the refrigerator.

The boys were in different schools in Massachusetts. David was in Jr High, about a mile away. Bobby went to the grade school just around the corner.

David came home one day and mentioned that one of his classmates was different. This was in the early days of desegragation and I thought the worst. The boy was black but that wasn't the difference. He had a Yankee accent and that was different to David. The black didn't seem to register.

We had been in Westover about a year and R. G. was notified that he would be transferred. Usually the Military keeps you about three years for economic reasons. Moving is expensive.

He was told it was a Movie job in Hawaii. That didn't sound so bad. He was told that he would have to volunteer since he had been in Westover such a short time. Rule of the Military: Never Volunteer for anything!

We ended up in Yokota, Japan. I enjoyed it. The move was confused from the beginning. We were told we couldn't go because we had not been eighteen months. The next day or so we were told we were going. This went on until there were not five working days to get the movers there. Some how we made it.

We had a tour of the country on the way. We drove to Virginia and visited Barbara and Ed. We saw the Skyline drive in Virginia. To stand on the trail and see three mountain ranges makes you feel small. Or you realize how large the country is!

We got to Tennessee and ate dinner at a small café near a river. We had the most delicious Cat Fish! We were all sick for months. R. G. couldn't get out of bed the next day. We stayed in the Motel an extra day and he felt he could drive. By this time the rest of us were sick. We got to Alabama and stopped at a Base Hospital. The Dr. looked sad and said he couldn't cure us but he could help the symptoms. He gave us huge bottles of some red stuff and we took that for weeks. It was a year before we were back to normal. The kindly Dr. explained that Cat Fish are bottom feeders and ours must have eaten something that poisoned us. I no longer eat Cat Fish.

We stopped in Loraine and visited R. G.'s parents. We stopped in Silverton and visited my Grandparents. We drove through New Mexico and Arizona. We visited Margaret and Glenn in Phoenix. Then on to San Francisco and the plane to Japan.

Driving through the desert was miserable. The cars in that day didn't have air conditioners. Rest Stops were a long way between. I felt so sorry for the poor Indians that lived there. I was evidently quite vocal about it. On our return I was quite pleased. Uranium had been discovered on the reservation and the Indians were not so poor!!

We got to San Francisco several days early to sight see. One trip in to town from the Air Base was enough. We saw all the tourist things. Fisherman's Warf, the trolleys, and were content to go back and wait for the plane.

R. G. turned the car in for shipment and we were all ready to fly.

We boarded the plane and all was well for a few hours. Just before the point of no return all the alarm bells went off and the plane turned back. The crew was assuring us the alarms had been set wrong and all was well. You could look out the window and see the shadow of the Amphibian plane on the clouds below. They were flying above and behind us so we couldn't see the plane. It was harder to hide the shadow.

We arrived back at Travis and were settled in the terminal to wait for repairs. We sat until late afternoon and boarded again.

This time we didn't get that far out when the alarms went off again. We couldn't see the plane following us but we could see the outboard engine was on fire. Back to Travis and a fast landing. One of the pilots on board said he didn't know you could make a fighter landing in a transport plane!

We were put up over night at a new Motel near the terminal. It had not been officially opened. We got a nights sleep and put on the same clothes in the morning.

Back to the terminal and loaded on the plane again. This time it was a different plane, not better, just different. For some reason several of the passengers couldn't be found for this trip.

We arrived at Tachikawa without incident.

Our sponsors met us and we were taken to the Guest Hotel for our first taste of Japan. We stayed there until we found housing on the Japanese economy.

Some Americans came to a foreign country and expected it to be just like Stateside. They did themselves a disservice. If they adapted to the country they had a good time and learned a lot.

Our Paddy house was a square house with a living room, kitchen, two bedrooms and a bathroom. The heat in the winter was provided by a heater made of a 50 gallon drum with a perforated steel cover. Worked fine after you learned a few tricks.

The bathroom had a tub about 6 feet long and 3 feet wide. It was tiled in small one inch tiles. The sides were straight up and down, not slanted like stateside.

We were given a list of furniture to bring. The base was just changing over to supplying furniture and appliances so we were told to bring little more than our clothes.

Kitchen ranges were on order but for the first few months we cooked on an electric, two level hot plate. The same kind of hot plate that resturants use for heating coffee. It is amazing what you can do with nothing when nothing is all you have.

The boat arrived about once a month to supply the commissary. You got it when it came or you did without. The economy had beautiful vegetables. The carrots were three feet long. We were told not to use them. Five thousand years of human fertilizer was a little hard for the American to get used to.   We did have a hydroponics farm to supply fresh vegetables so we did well.

Yokota had been a Japanese Military base. I often wondered what ghosts remained. Since the boys school in England was Eisenhours headquarters in WWII and their High School in Japan was a Kamikaze training school that has puzzled me, too.

Life was simplified in Japan. The sewer system was a concrete ditch. For the Americans a lid of concrete slabs was added. This made it easy to find the stoppage. You just lifted slabs until you found the problem. Of course it overflowed a little but that didn't matter when you remembered the soil was lava dust with generations of human fertilizer. A little more couldn't hurt.

At that time most of the wives sewed and had brought sewing machines. It didn't take long to be spoiled with the fabric. I have never seen brocade in the United States like we could purchase there. If they import it I have never seen it. There were all kinds of silks to be had. Every kind of fabric from sheer to coarse raw silk.

Raw silk is made from the outer part of the cocoon and is used like we use muslin. The American not knowing this used it for everything. The Japanese, not to be outdone, embroidered it and sewed chiffon and satin flowers on it. I still have some.

Our village was a silkworm growing area. There were large barns with shelves for the silkworms. These were kept supplied with the leaves to feed the larva until the cocoons were ready.

The fabric was woven and dyed and washed in the creeks. You would drive along and see yards of fabric floating in the water as the color set.

Children were told to drink tea if away from home. At least the water was boiled. That lead to another problem. The babies learned to drink green tea with the maids. By the time they got back to the States they thought that was all they could drink. That was before Green tea was popular and some Mothers had a problem.

Boy Scouts were popular. This was the year the World Jamboree was at Fuji. Both Boys had a great time. They climbed Fuji and met scouts from all over the world.

R. G. didn't have a lot of free time. This was while the fighting in Laos was still going on. History never mentions those years. Then the beginning of the Viet Nam conflict brought a lot of pressure to bear.

American Pilots have always been free spirits. Some of them couldn't resist straying into Chinese air space. They would come back with 35mm pictures taken with their personal cameras.

The equipment used in mapping and charting is not suitable for printing 35mm. I had taken my projector to Japan. In comparison to the million dollar mapping printers mine looked like it was made out of tomato cans. I would get a call asking to borrow my projector, take it to the Squadron and hand it over the fence. We finally solved the problem. They kept the projector and I borrowed it when I needed it. That saved a lot of trips.

With the boys in school and R. G. busy, I used to go to Yokahoma, Atsugi or some of the other military bases to shop. Atsugi was on the road to Yokahoma and had a nice BX. You can't keep from wondering years later about fate. President Kennedy's murderer was stationed at Atsugi at that time.

The U-2 was also stationed there. There was one incident when the plane crashed on take-off. The Japanese police got to the field first and took charge. The Military Police got there and declared it their business. That one turned out all right but it took the Diplomatic Corps to keep them from shooting each other. Another bit of history, that U-2 was repaired and sent to Turkey. That was the U-2 the Russians shot down!

Annie Bell
Bowie
Mary Belle
Badgett
Annabell
Patterson
Barbara
Bell
Maribel
Savage

36715

B.O.V.S. FORM B

Texas State Board of Health
BUREAU OF VITAL STATISTICS
STANDARD CERTIFICATE OF BIRTH

1045

PLACE OF BIRTH

County _Grayson_   Reg. Dis. No. __________   Register No. _408_

City _Sherman_ No. _3 N Middleton_ __________ Ward

(2) FULL NAME OF CHILD _Not Named_   (If child is not yet named, make supplemental report, as directed)

(3) Sex of Child	(4) Twin, triplet or other	(5) Number in order of birth	(12) Legitimate	(13) Date of Birth
Female	(To be answered in event of plural births)		Yes	6-22-26 (Month) (Day) (Year)

FATHER	MOTHER
(6) FULL NAME _Wm Payne Savage_	(14) FULL MAIDEN NAME _Marabul Bodgeh_
(7) RESIDENCE _Sherman Tex 23_	(15) RESIDENCE _Sherman Tex 20_
(8) COLOR _White_ AGE AT LAST BIRTHDAY 23 (Years)	(16) COLOR _White_ AGE AT LAST BIRTHDAY 20 (Years)
(9) BIRTHPLACE _Texas_	(17) BIRTHPLACE _Texas_
(10) OCCUPATION _Hardwick-Etter_	(18) OCCUPATION _House wife_
(11) Number of children born to this mother, prior to this birth 0	Number of children born of this mother now living

CERTIFICATE OF ATTENDING PHYSICIAN OR MIDWIFE*

(19) I hereby certify that I attended the birth of this child, who was _alive_ (Born Alive or Stillborn) 11.10 P. M. on the date above stated.

*When there was no attending physician or midwife, then the father, householder, etc., should make this return. A stillborn child is one that neither breathes nor shows other evidence of life after birth.

(Signature) _C. G. Struther M.D._
Sherman Tex (Physician or Midwife)

Given name added from a supplemental report __________, 19____

____
Registrar

Address __________
Filed JUN 23 1926 __________, 19____ _J. A. Kennedy_
Registrar

USE THIS FORM FOR CORRECTING A CERTIFICATE FILED AT THE TIME THE BIRTH OCCURRED. 36715
THIS FORM CANNOT BE USED FOR CORRECTING RECORDS FILED THROUGH THE PROBATE COURT

1. PLACE OF BIRTH
STATE OF TEXAS

TEXAS DEPARTMENT OF HEALTH
BUREAU OF VITAL STATISTICS
STANDARD CERTIFICATE OF BIRTH

COUNTY OF _Grayson_

CITY OR PRECINCT NO. _Sherman_

GIVE STREET AND NUMBER OR NAME OF INSTITUTION

2. FULL NAME OF CHILD _Maribel Savage_

RESIDENCE OF THE MOTHER — STREET AND NO. ______ CITY _Sherman_ COUNTY _Grayson_ STATE _Tex_

| 3. SEX | FOR PLURAL BIRTHS ONLY: | | 6. LEGITIMATE? | 7. DATE OF BIRTH |
| _Female_ | 4. TWIN, TRIPLET, OTHER | 5. NUMBER, IN ORDER OF BIRTH | _Yes_ | _June 22_, 19 _26_ |

FATHER

8. FULL NAME _William Payne Savage_

SOCIAL SECURITY NUMBER

9. POSTOFFICE ADDRESS _Sherman, Tex_

10. COLOR OR RACE _W_   11. AGE AT TIME OF THIS BIRTH _24_ (YEARS)

12. BIRTHPLACE (STATE OR COUNTRY) _Texas_

19A. TRADE, PROFESSION OR KIND OF WORK DONE _Hardware_

19B. INDUSTRY OR BUSINESS IN WHICH ENGAGED _Hardware_

20. NUMBER OF CHILDREN BORN TO THIS MOTHER INCLUDING THIS BIRTH _One_

SIGNATURE OF INFORMANT _C. R. Badgett_

MOTHER

14. FULL MAIDEN NAME _Maribel Badgett_

SOCIAL SECURITY NUMBER

15. POSTOFFICE ADDRESS _Sherman, Tex_

16. COLOR OR RACE _W_   17. AGE AT TIME OF THIS BIRTH _20_ (YEARS)

18. BIRTHPLACE (STATE OR COUNTRY) _Oklahoma_

19A. TRADE, PROFESSION OR KIND OF WORK DONE _Housewife_

19B. INDUSTRY OR BUSINESS IN WHICH ENGAGED

21. NUMBER OF CHILDREN BORN TO THIS MOTHER AND NOW LIVING _One_

ADDRESS OF INFORMANT _Silverton_   TEXAS

22. MEDICAL ATTENDANCE

I HEREBY CERTIFY TO THE BIRTH OF THIS CHILD BORN ALIVE / STILLBORN AT ______ M. ON THE ABOVE DATE

TEXAS DEPARTMENT OF HEALTH
FILED JUN 20 1952
BUREAU OF VITAL STATISTICS

AND THE PROPHYLACTIC USED TO PREVENT OPHTHALMIA NEONATORUM WAS

______ 19 ____   ____________   MIDWIFE / OTHER   POSTOFFICE ADDRESS   TEXAS
DATE   SIGNATURE

23. FILE NUMBER | FILE DATE _19_ | SIGNATURE OF LOCAL REGISTRAR | POSTOFFICE ADDRESS   TEXAS

AFFIDAVIT

STATE OF TEXAS
COUNTY OF _Briscoe_

Before me on this day appeared _C. R. Badgett_ known to me to be the person whose name is signed to the above certificate, who on oath deposes and says that the facts stated in the foregoing certificate are true and correct to the best of his/her knowledge and belief, and that this certificate is filed for the purpose of correcting the original record of the birth of _Baby Savage_

(Name appearing on original certificate)

Signature _C. R. Badgett_

Sworn to and subscribed before me, this _22_ day of _May_, 19 _53_.

C. E. Anderson

Notary Public in and for _Briscoe_ County, Texas.

www.ingramcontent.com/pod-product-compliance
Lightning Source LLC
Chambersburg PA
CBHW080820280726
48660CB00018B/3553